Gambit Publishing

Chicago, IL


Library of Congress Control Number: 2001091933
Hiller, Matt, 1977-
        Are You Hardcore?! : 316 ways to tell you're obsessed with professional wrestling / Matt Hiller and Joe Lisi.
        p. cm.
        ISBN 0-967591-7-24
1. Wrestling—Humor. 2. Wrestling—United States. I. Lisi, Joe, 1977-  II. Title.




Library of Congress cataloging by Dennis R. McGuire.

# 316

## Ways to Tell You're

## OBSESSED
## OBSESSED
## OBSESSED

## with Professional Wrestling!

**By Matt Hiller and Joe Lisi**

*Gambit Publishing*
*Chicago, Illinois*

## *Special Thanks*

Brian "B.C." Coulombe: Huge thanks to B.C. for being our comedy guinea pig. If he didn't laugh - or at the very least smirk - at a joke, we didn't put it in the book. He even came up with a few jokes of his own which got sprinkled in. Did I mention he's done Senton Bombs off the top of his garage? That ought to get him over with you guys.

Justin Jones: Another huge thanks goes out to Justin! He's a fun and crazy guy to work with, not to mention he can steam a blouse like nobody's business! Without his intense computer savvy and helpfulness we literally couldn't have gotten the book to the publisher.

Vince McMahon: We couldn't make a special thanks list without the King of Sports Entertainment himself! Without him not only would we have nothing to do Monday or Thursday, this book could not have been made! This guy's probably had more influence on us than some of our relatives. Oh yeah, can you give us jobs? THANK YOU VINCE!

# Foreword

You're watching wrestling. We're watching wrestling. Hell, I bet somewhere Rick "The Model" Martel is watching wrestling. It was ingrained into you as a child. We all remember those sweet Saturday mornings that started off with Pee Wee's Funhouse and took you straight past noon with two solid hours of pure sports entertainment. Although, back then you thought it was just "wrestling". Well, now wrestling has exploded, and changed. Gone are the days of the self-loving "Adorable" Adrian Adonis, the jolly yet brash sailor "Tugboat", and the parrot-toting Koko B Ware! Gone, maybe. Forgotten, never!

We all hold a special place for classic wrestlers, and many of us can recall their careers in vivid detail. Well, it's the 21st century and wrestling has definitely evolved and it's kicking ass. The action is hotter, the story lines are better, and the wrestlers themselves are just as much actors as they are athletes. Wrestling is so good in fact; many of us haven't left the house on a Monday or Thursday in years. On what other show can you see a man eat his own dog, an 80 year-old woman fly through a table, or a man get crushed inside a car, all LIVE? That shit's not happening on "Friends!"

Face it, you're obsessed, but that's cool. Recently, Joe and I realized we were also obsessed which is why we wrote this book. In here you'll find many ideas, thoughts, scenarios, and references that truly addicted wrestling fans have had or can identify with. OK, some are just crazy ones we made up, but it's all good. Whether you're an old-school fan, a new post-Stone Cold fan, or an Internet smart fan, there's stuff in here you're gonna seriously laugh at as you realize just how much you know about wrestling! Do you remember freaking the hell out at Royal Rumble 1989 where Ax and Smash drew numbers 1 and 2? Us too. Have you "guaran-damn-teed" anything this week? Or have you ever incited an "ASS-HOLE" chant during a movie? You probably have. So grab this book and some beer, and see just how obsessed you and your friends are!

*From Matt*

I think first off I need to thank me. I'm hands down one of the top guys I know and I couldn't have done it without me. Also thanks to **Mom and Dad** for getting me the King Kong Bundy and Greg Valentine figures and surprising me with them DURING school for no reason at all. Thanks to **Twiggy Nana** and **Papa**, **Nicky Nana** and **Papa**, **Nate**, **Chris** and the rest of the family. Also **Akilia "Ang" Flanagan**, **Jeff Palumbo** who I've been chillin' with since we were babies, and **Christina**, the e-mail princess!

*From Joe*

I would like to thank **my parents** for getting me into wrestling, and the rest of my family (**Mike**, **Denise**, **Chiara**, **Noah**, **Nick**, **Kris**, **Ian**, **Sue**, **John** and **Gram**) for putting up with me talking about it all the time. I would also like to thank **Beau**, who is one of the coolest people I know. Lastly, thanks to **Jessie**, **Kiana**, **Natalie**, **Cameron**, **Tammy**, and **Jenny** for all being pretty cool people and for all the free movies.

# You Know You're Obsessed with Wrestling When...

**1** You attempt to steal someone's girlfriend by asking her to be your business advisor.

**2** Whenever lights are turned on you raise your outstretched arms slowly as if you are controlling them with your mind.

**3** Instead of referring to yourself as unemployed, you say you're character is under creative development.

**4** You go to a stunt show and after every stunt chant HO-LY Shit, HO-LY Shit!

**5** You always enter a room with a water bottle, pour some over your head and then spit some water out.

**6** After getting hired for a new job you quickly film a few vignettes to be shown in the few weeks before your first day.

**7** Instead of saying you have an interview you say you are having a dark match.

**8** You run over your biggest rival at work with a car.

**9** At Japanese restaurants you are paranoid someone will throw salt in your eyes.

**10** You go to a lumberyard and every time someone picks up a 2x4 you yell Hooooooo!

**11** When someone shows you puppies you're like "hey, those aren't puppies".

**12** When your little son is crying hysterically from just skinning his knee you scold him for "overselling".

**13** You refer to your girlfriend breaking up with you as her "heel turn".

**14** During a championship game you get

hit with the softball and then "blade" for drama and crowd concern.

**15** You know exactly what cities the Ice Palace, Gund Arena, and National Car Rental Arena are in.

**16** You recognize the name Ted Arcidi.

**17** You organize a witty wrestling newsletter you cleverly titled "Tag Ropes".

**18** Instead of asking to be seated in a restaurant, you chant "TA-BLE, TA-BLE!".

**19** There are rubber bands in your facial hair.

**20** Before doing something bad, you first look all around for GTV.

**21** You pass a car accident and chant "E C DUB! E C DUB!

**22** You think the guy down your street who

lost his leg in Vietnam is "hardcore".

**23** You refer to the people you don't know as "jobbers".

**24** A usual Sunday morning is waking up in a strange house with an empty 12 pack of Keystone Light and some old Shotgun Saturday Night tapes.

**25** To you, the American Revolution was nothing more than a long feud with a title change.

**26** You own 2 or more items made of Spandex, and wear them under your clothes just in case.

**27** You won't date a girl unless you're absolutely sure she can do a hurricanrana.

**28** You always carry blood capsules in case you need to sell an internal injury.

**29** Before you go on vacation you have

someone attack you at your job to
explain your absence.

**30** You have your own catch phrase printed
on a T-shirt (that only you wear).

**31** Whenever you watch the Friday The
13th movies, every time Jason comes
on screen you start an Asshole chant.

**32** The only cologne you wear is Arrogance.

**33** You always answer the phone Hey, Yo!

**34** Whenever you play a board game, just
before you are about to lose you hit the
other players with a chair so they only
get a cheap DQ victory.

**35** You wonder if Chris Benoit will coordi-
nate the color of his tights with the
color of the ring ropes.

**36** The only wonders of the world you
know of are the 8th and 9th.

**37** To this day, you still say your prayers AND eat your vitamins.

**38** You know who H-Bloxx are.

**39** You use words like sucktitude, awe-someness, and heinousity in everyday conversation.

**40** Every time someone screams WAAAZZZAAAPPP! you head butt someone in the groin.

**41** You argue with your best friend about which one of you is the Shawn Michaels and which one is the Marty Janetty.

**42** Every time you're at a graduation ceremony you go from extreme excite-ment to severe anger as you realize that Macho Man Randy Savage is actually not there.

**43** When someone asks you where you are from you tell them Parts Unknown.

*"**46** When delivering a eulogy, you don't see the problem in equating death to being pinned by God."*

**44** You own Mr. Nanny, Suburban Commando, and 3 Ninjas: High Noon at Mega Mountain on video.

**45** You hire a person to throw you beers whenever you want one.

**46** When delivering a eulogy, you don't see the problem in equating death to being pinned by God.

**47** You won't associate with anyone who can't name all of the members of the Heenan Family.

**48** You reschedule flights, surgeries, funerals, and any other important engagement so as to not interfere with the big 5.

**49** Against your parents' wishes, you choose The Rock as your confirmation name.

**50** You divided all the fish in your tank

into tag teams, complete with tiny belts.

**51** When at a live wrestling event, you recite the commercials that would be on, had you been watching it at home.

**52** All your pick-up lines have the phrase "genetic jackhammer" in them.

**53** You consider giving your opinion a shoot.

**54** You fixed it so pyro goes off as you walk out your front door.

**55** You write poems on Frisbees.

**56** You still wonder what happened with the WBF.

**57** You white out the months on your calendar and replace them with the PPV names.

**58** When asked when Easter is you say "two weeks after Wrestlemania".

**59** You can't bring yourself to throw away your Akeem boxer shorts.

**60** You are still boycotting ABC over the cancellation of "Rockin Wrestling".

**61** You have at one time or another pushed 2 couches together to form a makeshift ring.

**62** You have tried each and every submission move on your sister to see if they really work.

**63** You know enough to never try to attack a guy that your friend is constraining for you.

**64** You still actively buy and use ICO PRO.

**65** You have 2 Smash figures because it was the only way to get Crush.

**66** You can easily discern "New Haircut Andre" from "Old Haircut Andre".

**67** You remember making tassels for your arms and boots from neon shoelaces.

**68** You can name each referee and put them in order of seniority.

**69** You bring signs to a house show.

**70** Whenever a wrestler comes out with a flag other than the U.S., you believe that country is an enemy and suddenly develop a sense of national pride.

**71** You begin every question you ask with "Whatcha gonna do when"...

**72** You knock out one of your front teeth to look more sadistic.

**73** You consider yourself the undiscovered fourth member of "Team Extreme".

**74** You have a reoccurring dream about kicking X-Pac's ass.

**75** Your mother hides the tables when you come over.

**76** You are still waiting for the WWF to bring back the "In Your House" PPVs in hopes that you will actually win the house this time.

**77** You ran out of the room crying when Tugboat turned heel.

**78** You are still trying to figure out a way to do a swanton bomb off of your roof without dying.

**79** You go to bullfights specifically to see the greatest bullfighter of them all, El Matador. Tito Santana.

**80** Whenever you see an old man walking with a cane, you chuckle to yourself and imagine him walking with a 7-foot masked man.

**81** You hold up signs for Raw and Smackdown, which you watch in your living room.

**82** You are able to argue at length about

why Damian was a much better snake than Lucifer.

**83** In order to make sure someone is asleep, you raise their arm three times, if it falls all three times, you know they are.

**84** You regard the Royal Rumble 1989, when Ax and Smash of Demolition drew numbers 1 and 2, as one of the best moments in your life.

**85** You know Vince McMahon's middle name.

**86** You read "Positively Page".

**87** You dream of the day when "Iron" Mike Sharp and Jose Louis Rivera make their triumphant return to the WWF.

**88** You sent Matilda a get well card.

**89** Every time the lights go out, when they come back on the person next to you is covered in mysterious red liquid.

**90** You have a pet parrot named Frankie.

**91** You refer to your basement as "The Dungeon".

**92** You call your parents Stu and Helen.

**93** You have written to the Emergency Broadcast System asking them to change their test from those annoying beeps to just playing Tests theme music.

**94** Instead of stairs, you have a circular-moving platform surrounded by fire in your house.

**95** You know all the words to the Russian National Anthem.

**96** You believe that everyone at the IRS dresses and acts like Irwin R. Shyster.

**97** You never trust anyone named McMahon (including the McMahons that live next door to you and America's sidekick, Ed McMahon).

**98** You fully understand HHH's "Game Over" shirt.

**99** Still buy green apple blowpops to get a green tongue.

**100** You always carry a microphone, and pace and hand gesture when you need to say something.

**101** You remember shouting "PUPPIES!" after seeing Mae Young's breasts, instead of feeling utter disgust.

**102** When engaging in small talk, your big opener is "Oh my God, did you see Raw?"

**103** You know how many quarters you have to put in the sticker machine before you get anyone other than a Stone Cold.

**104** You have caught yourself watching Battledome when there was no wrestling on.

**105** You laugh hysterically as you see a stocky 12-year-old girl in an orange bathing suit strutting with a black towel over her head.

**106** When your girlfriend tries to take an interest and asks if Jerry "The King" Lawler is King of The Ring, you just sigh with disgust.

**107** You and your friends know how much wrestlers' contracts are for, and regularly debate as to whether the company is getting their money's worth.

**108** You know a joke where the punch line is "cuz New Diesel said so!"

**109** You thought a sweet tag team would be Greg Valentine and Nailz, for obvious reasons, and later thought they could be called "Tools of the Trade".

**110** You've slammed your friend onto a cookie sheet of dog shit over a friendly argument.

**"114** *When someone tells you they saw a 3D movie, you become angry claiming that if the Dudley Boyz made a movie, you would sure as hell know about it.*"

**111** You operate a "protection agency" within your circle of friends.

**112** No matter how bad the situation, you never stray from the 3 L's.

**113** You know whether the mood has changed or not.

**114** When someone tells you they saw a 3D movie, you become angry claiming that if the Dudley Boyz made a movie, you would sure as hell know about it.

**115** When your dad dozes off, you quickly put on your pink pants and cut his hair.

**116** Tony Chimel is a household name.

**117** You shaved your "Anvil" beard last year, and regret it everyday.

**118** When you got married, you insisted "The Wedding March" be replaced with "BAM! BAM!" Bigelow's song.

**119** Whenever you put on your sunglasses, you do a brief dance.

**120** At work, you get your manager a megaphone for Christmas.

**121** You think no smoking signs are totally ripping off the RTC logo.

**122** You notice that Stephanie is at her most vulnerable when her hair is straight (or her hair gets curly when she's bad).

**123** When someone gets in the backseat you yell "WHERE TO_____-anie??" filling in the blank with their name.

**124** You gain an excessive amount of weight until you can do a respectable stinkface.

**125** You know that Steve Austin and Trish Stratus have the same birthday, and hold a small celebration at home.

**126** You sob as you recall the progression of the legendary Road Warriors to Legion of Doom, and sadly, to LOD 2000.

**127** You began heavily eating overstuffed ravioli in 1999.

**128** Every 4th Sunday you're torn between the PPV pre-show and "Sunday Night Heat."

**129** You know exactly how much Big Show weighs from week to week.

**130** You have a wrestling themed beach towel tacked to your wall.

**131** You liked "Aggression".

**132** You theorize about the amount of ass the child of Chyna and HHH would kick.

**133** You think that no one in Japan and the Island countries wear shoes.

**134** You think that Skinner should sue the Crocodile Hunter for gimmick infringement.

**135** When you go to a funeral you just assume that the person in the coffin lost a casket match.

**136** You watched Hulk Hogan's E! True Hollywood Story.

**137** You had fangs surgically implanted in your teeth.

**138** You are still waiting for the lab results to see if the pictures Ric Flair had of him with Elizabeth were real or not.

**139** All of your socks have faces drawn on the ends of them.

**140** You end every conversation with "And that's an order!", despite having no military background.

**141** You always arrive at work about an hour late because you feel you are a main-eventer.

**142** You named your son Little Beaver and encouraged your other fat son to jump on him, but find it less and less cool as they grow up.

**143** After you win a fight, you stuff a dollar bill in the other person's mouth.

**144** You can name all of Dean Malenkos' 1000 moves.

**145** You tag the guy coming out of the public restroom before you go in.

**146** You never need to call somebody, because your ass knows.

**147** You've constructed a championship belt for the family Scrabble game.

**148** Before beginning anything you tear off your t-shirt.

**149** You either own or have interest in buying a power-giving urn.

**150** There are always trash can lids, bamboo rods, and banquet tables hidden under your bed.

**151** This year, your birthday cake was shaped like someone applying the camel clutch.

**152** You have a gym membership just because you know the wrestlers workout there when they have a show in town.

**153** You know what the inside of a turnbuckle looks and tastes like.

**154** You brag about how well you took the "bump" when you fell painting.

**155** You do an unexpected heel turn on your best friend, then try to justify it by explaining that your reason for doing so is because he was "holding you back."

**156** You arrive at school or work in a mysterious black limousine, and get out surrounded by security guards.

**157** You win all your matches against your little brother by DQ because your mother interferes on his behalf.

**158** You keep calling all your local retailers to see if they carry Rikishi Phatware.

**159** Unfortunately, you know what your own dog tastes like.

**160** When signing something, you leave out your last name and replace it with "the giant."

**161** You enthusiastically yell "Off the top!", when you jump off of anything, no matter how small.

**162** Your kids' names are Stephanie and Shane.

**163** You can recall, with gusto, each Haiti Kid match.

**164** When someone tells you they lost their belt you reply "damn, who to?"

**165** You know all the good seating sections in each arena in your entire state.

**166** You know the life span of a Spanish announce table is approximately 1 hour and 55 minutes.

**167** You think you're funny because you named your bowling team "The Pinfalls".

**168** You wear heavily worn, outdated wrestling T-shirts, which no longer fit, to events so people know you're old-school, not bandwagon.

**169** Each Monday you religiously order your food at 8:20 pm so it will definitely be there by 9. And you know the delivery guy.

**170** You can easily predict the upcoming match by seeing a Slam of the Week clip.

**171** You know where the phrase "a little

**"176** *You consider the promotion you got at work your much deserved push."*

tight one can stop me on a dime" is from.

**172** You have more foam fingers than you do real fingers.

**173** You don't think of the term "ho" as overly derogatory, in fact you think saying a girl looks like a ho is a compliment.

**174** You are still waiting to find out who IS the "sharpest knife in the drawer".

**175** Your favorite musicians are still Alice Cooper and Cyndi Lauper.

**176** You consider the promotion you got at work your much deserved push.

**177** You call everyone "BROTHER!", even women.

**178** You know the home city and state of each wrestler, but aren't sure what cities your parents were born in.

**179** You can give the "combined" weight of any 2 wrestlers, regardless if they're a tag team or not.

**180** You know who Jean-Paul and Dwayne are.

**181** You can easily tell Dave and Earl Hebner apart.

**182** You have bought magazines and watched shows that you normally wouldn't have because they featured wrestlers.

**183** You call your boss Vince, regardless of what his/her name is.

**184** You bought a piece of land so you could build and live on "Know Your Role Blvd.".

**185** You have a petition going to get Webster's to add Roodypoo, Heinousity, Slapnuts and Puppies to the dictionary.

**186** You dressed in formal wear while watching Test and Stephanie's wedding from home.

**187** When you are asked to be a pallbearer at your uncle's funeral, you reply "Listen, there is only one Paul Bearer, and I think an impersonation of him would just be in bad taste."

**188** You cut out the sides of all your T-shirts so you have the "tough guy" poncho look.

**189** You visit wwf.com at least twice a day, and are able to pick Big Country out of a crowd.

**190** You have been to more than one live wrestling show in one week. (We've done 3, can you beat that?)

**191** You have planned out exactly what you would say to every wrestler if you ever happen to meet them in person.

**192** When a party slows down, you always

suggest a battle royal.

**193** Regardless of the weather, you're never wearing a shirt.

**194** Instead of a simple "yes" you always answer "OHHHHHH YEEEEEEAAAAAHHH."

**195** You remember which team won when the wrestlers were on Family Feud.

**196** You notice a direct correlation between a wrestler getting a haircut, and getting a "push" and a new storyline.

**197** You always keep a sock down your pants, for different reasons.

**198** You watch a lot of C-Span just in case Jesse Ventura cuts a promo.

**199** You have read and enjoyed the Undertaker comic book series.

**200** You know there is a male and a female Gorgeous George.

**"205** *You end phone calls and sign letters 'bye bye, jack-ass'."*

**201** You have stopped saying "guarantee" altogether, and now only say "guaran-damn-tee".

**202** You give a wink, sly smile and say "you bet I do" when someone asks if you want pie.

**203** You are still reeling from when you found out Jack Tunney wasn't the REAL President of the WWF.

**204** At events, you bring a sign for a mid-card wrestler in your own personal quest to get him "over."

**205** You end phone calls and sign letters "bye bye, jackass".

**206** The first thing you show people when they come to your house is your "ultra rare mint condition, signed, framed Beverly Brothers poster".

**207** You've had to move more than three times in the last year because you keep adding a "Loser Leaves Town" stipulation to your pick-up games of basketball.

**208** You ask your boss to pair you with a beautiful woman so you can get over faster.

**209** You can name every person that played Doink the Clown in — order.

**210** You would vote for Vince McMahon if he ran for president.

**211** The main ingredient in everything you cook is J.R.'s BBQ sauce.

**212** You call your girlfriend Mamacita.

**213** When in the mall, you chuckle to yourself every time you pass The People's Pottery.

**214** On New Year's Eve 1999, you watched "Eve of Destruction" instead of watching the ball drop in Times Square.

**215** You sit through every concert you go to wondering why the guy with the guitar doesn't hit someone over the head with it. What else is there to do with a guitar?

**216** You still wonder why Mr. Fuji would leave the WWF just to start up a film company, but you are happy that he has been so successful.

**217** You know all the words to all the songs on "Piledriver", the album.

**218** As far as you're concerned, there is only one Vader, and he isn't Luke's father.

**219** Unlike everyone else, you are happy when it's Monday.

**220** As far as you're concerned, next to a diamond, a Samoan's head is the hardest surface on the earth.

**221** You use your middle finger to greet friends, wave goodbye, as well as a proudly salute and it's not the least bit offensive to you.

**222** When your fiancee reminds you of your rehearsal wedding dinner you say "What is that? Like a house show?"

**223** When you enter a room, the first thing you do is slap your own personal logo on the door. When anyone knocks you say, "If it's Kevin Kelly I'm not here!"

**224** You've twice staged your own steroid scandal.

**225** You've put a few cats inside a guinea pig cage for a makeshift Hell in the Cell.

**226** You know that "great in-ring technician" is wrestling speak for "no mic skills or charisma".

**227** After returning to work from a long

absence you blame your non-produc-
tivity on ring rust.

**228** You thought about tattooing your
girlfriend's name on your throat.

**229** You think it's cool when you get hit
with beer at a live show.

**230** You've shed tears at the dramatic Hulk
Hogan/Mark Pellegrino hospital room
scene in "No Holds Barred."

**231** You constantly complain about how
refs should go back to wearing bow
ties.

**232** For each room in your house, you've
installed ring posts in the corners.

**233** You don't care what anybody's name
is.

**234** Whenever you spit your gum out, you
make a conscious effort to slap it in
mid-air.

**235** You aren't Scottish, but own a kilt.

**236** You consider people who don't know the real names of masked wrestlers vastly inferior to yourself.

**237** You felt disappointed and misled after renting "The Godfather."

**238** You are not from Minnesota but have a "my governor can beat up your governor" bumper sticker.

**239** You can effortlessly pick former Bushwacker manager "Jameson" out of a lineup.

**240** You have worn elbow or knee pads in public.

**241** At some point, you've regarded Elizabeth as the most beautiful woman in the world.

**242** You have Chyna's Playboy photos as the desktop wallpaper on the family computer.

**243** When casual old school fans remark about how cool "Pipers Pit" and "The Funeral Parlor" were, you bring up your love for Adrian Adonis' "The Flower Shop" just to one-up them.

**244** You have an old Junkyard Dog promo as your voice mail greeting.

**245** You remember thinking how awesome Virgil would be if he wrestled, and then remember being wrong.

**246** You bombard your local radio stations with requests for "Get Rowdy".

**247** You and your wife try to conceive each July in hopes of a Wrestlemania baby.

**248** You can name all the wrestlers who got the sleeper to work.

**249** You once took an exotic cruise to the Isle of Tonga specifically to see where Haku grew up.

**250** You read the Murder on the Orient Express and to your surprise, there was absolutely no mention of Kato or Tanaka.

**251** You have signed a yearbook "NWO 4LIFE".

**252** You have been laughed at in Student Council after suggesting separate facilities for Red and White NWO.

**253** You always secretly felt the Natural Disasters would have been a more complete and effective stable with the addition of The Texas Tornado.

**254** At some time, you have had a fantasy daydream where Vince McMahon gives you a Willy Wonka style tour of the WWF Headquarters, showing you classic props and costumes from wrestling past.

**255** Regardless of their size, you often draw attention to your biceps by kissing them.

**256** You have no qualms about dousing people in beer.

**257** You were pissed after seeing the play "The King And I", because not only was JR not in it, it was a totally different King.

**258** You think the current election process should be replaced by one in which everyone in each state gathers in one spot while the moderator yells out, "If you think _____ should be president, give me a hell yeah!" Then the winner is based on the response.

**259** You go into a record store and are astounded to find out that not only has Sting had a great wrestling career, but a very successful recording career as well.

**260** You do a run-in at your local high school wrestling meet by hitting your friend's opponent with a chair.

**261** You are still mad at yourself for over-sleeping on the day that the Lex Express passed through your town.

**262** After you get fired from your job you call your boss's wife in an attempt to get her to rehire you behind his back.

**263** You offer people money to do degrading things, like licking your feet or eating dog food, just to again prove your point that everyone has a price.

**264** You've either been hit or hit someone with a flaming weapon.

**265** You carry a sign with your name and a large arrow pointing down written on it everywhere you go.

**266** You note wrestlers' birthdays on your calendar.

**267** You spend all your time trying to get on "Who Wants to Be a Millionaire" in hopes you will win the million dollars and can enter the WWF as the new Million Dollar Man.

**268** You make it a point to get arrested in Cobb County, Georgia just to meet the Big Boss Man.

**269** You're still trying to get your girlfriend to wear a bubble wrap bikini.

**270** You've gone to all your local porn shops and searched the entire Internet for the movies "The Preacher's Wife" and "Saving Ryan's Privates" starring Val Venis.

**271** You and two of your friends wear sweater vests and changed your names to Rodney, Pete Gas, and Joey Abs.

**272** The only word you say is "Indeed!"

**273** Every time you say a two-word phrase or statement, you preface it with "I've got two words for you!"

**274** On more than one occasion, you've had dreams in which you are good friends with various wrestlers.

**275** Whenever a girl you don't like starts talking, you begin a Slut chant, then power-bomb her through a table.

**276** You named your dog Joey Numbers.

**277** You swear your garbage man is former WWF superstar Duke "The Dumpster" Drosey.

**278** You still contend that given the right push, Maestro and Symphony could have been the top heel couple in the business.

**279** You bought Tammy Lynn Stychs breast implant.

**280** You believe that Hulk Hogan's defeat of Sergeant Slaughter was a turning point of the Persian Gulf War.

**281** After drinking a glass of Don Fino wine, you say "Mmm, that's sensational sherry!, then laugh to yourself.

**282** For your grandpa's funeral you decided wearing your "Rattlesnake" t-shirt was much more appropriate than your "Smokin Skull' shirt.

**283** You incessantly play-by-play everything going on around you.

**284** You own and maintain the Official Flash Funk web site.

**285** You have been caught cutting up mom's old bathing suits to make yourself a singlet.

**286** For the life of you, you can't remember what you did on Thursdays before Smackdown premiered.

**287** You read the Smackdown spoilers Tuesday then bet on the match outcomes with unsuspecting friends.

**288** Most or all of your e-mail addresses, screen names, and passwords are wrestling-related.

**289** You've been pissed because they've made 6 different Bob Holly figures, but still haven't made a Mideon, Essa Rios, or especially, Linda.

**290** You are pissed at the Phantom of the Opera guy for totally ripping off Warlords face mask.

**291** You are constantly trying to convince women to settle their differences in a Bra and Panties match.

**292** When you turn off your TV, you can see a faint image of the WWF and USA network logos burned in the corners.

**293** The title of your final in English was "Why the Fabulous Freebirds Were Neither Fabulous, Nor Free."

**294** You started wearing your Bushwhackers shirt again because now that you're older, you think its funny sexual innuendo.

**295** On your mailbox, instead of your last name you have "Worlds Most Dangerous Man."

**296** When a match comes on, you call each move 3 seconds before it happens.

**297** WWF Wrestlers start recognizing you in the crowd.

**298** The word ass is bleeped out when you speak.

**299** You start to chokeslam garbage into your trash can.

**300** Tiny Undertaker and Hardy Boyz symbols are scribbled in the margins of your notebook.

**301** The best compliment you ever gave your girlfriend is "Honey, I love you just as much as Lita."

**302** You notice that during a Royal Rumble the simple task of throwing a guy out of the ring becomes 10 times more difficult, sometimes requiring 3 guys to lift up one.

**303** You plan to honeymoon aboard the Wrestle Vessel.

**304** You wear a W.W.J.Y.D.D.? bracelet, (of course meaning "What Would Junk Yard Dog Do?") to get you through the tough times.

**305** You know a disqualification is imminent anytime there is a guest commentator.

**306** You know the cause of death for more than 3 deceased wrestlers.

**307** You have gotten angered and frustrated while trying to make sense of the Bret Hart screwjob.

**308** After you were assigned a paper on a famous Frenchman, you didn't understand why your teacher wouldn't let you do it on Frenchy Martin.

**309** When you went to Memphis, TN, you were surprised to see how popular The Honky Tonk Man still is.

**310** You still sleep with your Mine doll.

**311** You understood or related to at least half of these signs that you are obsessed with wrestling.

**312** When it's dress down day at work you're like "Cool! No DQ!".

**313** You bought a bamboo tree so you could grow your own Kendo Sticks.

**314** Your speed dial has the number to order Pay-Per-Views,but not the fire department.

**315** You rigged up 2 TV's so you could watch WWF Raw and the final episode of WCW Nitro at the same time.(we sure as hell did!)

**316** You threw beer at your TV out of sheer

rage after seeing "Stone Cold" Steve Austin turn heel at Wrestlemania 17 - you subsequently went into a tirade about the creative direction of the WWF.Settle down man, - you're obsessed!

# Glossary

## "Blade/Blading

*Term for when a wrestler cuts himself with a concealed (or sometimes not so concealed) razor blade to make an injury look worse, like after being hit with a chair or the ring bell."*

# A

**"A little tight one can stop me on a dime"**
Hilarious lyric from "Mr. Ass" Billy Gunn's
theme music which can only be clearly
heard and appreciated on "WWF: The
Music Vol".

**"Aggression"** A rap remix CD of wrestlers
theme songs. We think it sucked and you
should too.

**Akeem** This big man was pretty much a
joke for most of his stay in the WWF.
When he first entered he was known as the
One Man Gang, a very large biker with a
mohawk. However, for a reason only Vince
will ever know, his gimmick changed to a
very overweight white guy claiming he was
from Africa. He wore a large yellow shirt
with blue trunks and was managed by
Slick. He did have a rather successful run as
one half of the Twin Towers with the Big
Bossman.

**Alice Cooper** A special celebrity guest at
Wrestlemania III, accompanying Jake "The

Snake" Roberts to the ring for his match against the Honky Tonk Man. On a side note, Matt met Alice in the mall once and got his autograph on a Dentyne Ice box.

**"Anvil beard"** Pointy, triangle chin beard made popular by Jim "the Anvil" Neidhardt. Did we say, "made popular"? We meant "worn".

**Arrogance** Awesome blinding fragrance used by Rick ìthe Modelî Martel. Did anyone else ever wonder why he stored it in one of those Bugs Bunny-ish spray containers?

**B**

**Bam Bam Bigelow** Everyone remembers this big man of the 90's. He had the size, the agility, and the tattooed head, basically everything someone needs to really make it in the business. But, for some reason, Bam Bam never did. Although he enjoyed moderate success in the WWF, his career there was basically over when he had to put over Lawrence Taylor at Wrestlemania XI.

He has since jumped to WCW.

**BattleDome** A show (which airs very late at night) that is a mix of wrestling, American Gladiators, and Double Dare. Recently, WCW attempted a crossover with the stars of BattleDome, remember? Neither does anyone else. On a side note, Joe's sister knows "Cuda".

**Beverly Brothers** A goofy-ass purple-clad tag team in the late 80's to early 90's, known for their beautiful blonde hair. They were managed by "The Genius".

**Big Country** Also known as BC, he does the daily news clips on WWF.com.

**Big 5** Term used for the original 5 Pay-Per-View events. They include Royal Rumble, Wrestlemania, King of the Ring, SummerSlam, and Survivor Series. People in the first 8 rows at these shows get to keep the chair they sit in, which is specially made for the event. However, tickets for these seats are around $300 each.

**Blade/Blading**  Term for when a wrestler cuts himself with a concealed (or sometimes not so concealed) razor blade to make an injury look worse, like after being hit with a chair or the ring bell.

**Bret Hart Screwjob**  This description could be a whole book by itself. In fact there is a whole movie about it,"Bret Hart: Wrestling with Shadows". So if you dont already know about this rent the movie or go visit http://www.rajahwwf.com/wwf/other/97screwjob.htm. That gives a great description of it.

**Bubble-wrap Bikini**  Worn by the WWF's resident exhibitionist "The Kat" at Royal Rumble 2000 during the Miss Royal Rumble Bikini contest. There is a company now whose only business is making bubble-wrap clothing.

**Bump**  A big fall during a match, or just a violent hit, like being put through a table. Mick Foley's fall from the top of the Hell in the Cell cage at King of the Ring 1998 is regarded as one of the biggest bumps of all time.

**Bushwhackers**  These old, crazy, Australian cousins with barely a full set of teeth between them were more or less comic relief.  Butch and Luke were never a serious threat to the tag titles scene and never held the belts. They did do that cool thing with their arms though.

**Business Advisor**  Stephanie McMahon-Helmsley's title when she was managing Kurt Angle's career; against HHHs wishes, mind you.

## C

**Camel Clutch**  Vicious submission move made famous by the Iron Sheik and Sergeant Slaughter.  Fun Fact: The Sheik was actually on the Jerry Springer show, not as a celebrity guest but because he was involved in a love triangle! Leave it to the Sheik!

**Confirmation Name**  This term isn't

wrestling-related at all, but for those of you non-religious people out there, we thought we would enlighten you. In the Catholic religion, when you get the sacrament of Confirmation, you choose a name. Since we are not theologians, we have no idea why this is done, but it is.

**Cyndi Lauper** A celebrity guest at the first Wrestlemania. She accompanied Wendi Richter to the ring for her Woman's title match against Lelani Kai, and helped her take home the title. Also during this time, Cyndi put famed WWF manager, Captain Lou Albano, in her music video for "Girls Just Wanna Have Fun", playing her father.

## D

**Dave Hebner** Identical twin brother of senior official, Earl Hebner. He is also known as the man that screwed Hulk Hogan out of the title on Saturday Night's Main Event, when he was paid off by the Million Dollar Man to pose as his brother Earl and fast-count Hogan. It was later revealed that Dave was an imposter. He is now a Road Agent for the WWF, travelling with the wrestlers and helping out back-stage.

**Damian**  Jake "The Snake" Roberts first, and BEST, snake. We dont care what you say; you have to respect Damian's work.

**Dark Match**  A match that takes place before the televised matches begin to warm up the crowd.  They usually involve new up-and-coming talent most people haven't heard of yet.  Joe saw Undertaker and Ultimate Warrior in dark matches before they made their official television debuts.

**Doink the Clown**  This sometimes fun-loving, sometimes demonic, clown/wrestler was a staple of the early to mid-90's.  He was known for his ringside antics which included a water-squirting flower on his lapel, a bucket of confetti, and the ability to multiply.  Throughout the tenure of Doink the clown, five different wrestlers took on the role. Don't worry, we didn't notice either.

## "Eve of Destruction

*Who needs Dick Clark and his balls? This special highlight show of 1999 aired opposite the New Years Eve special in Times Square. At midnight Y2J Chris Jericho treated us to a cool promo."*

**Don Fino wine** Another non-wrestling term, but again we thought we would educate you a little bit. According to what I read on the Internet, a Don Fino is a superior fino Sherry with a pale yellow straw color, with shades of green and gold; It is very pungent smelling from long maturing under flourescent light, fresh and delicate. Very dry finish. Consider yourself a wine connoisseur.

**Duke "The Dumpster" Drosey** Wow! What was Vince thinking? This guy's gimmick was a GARBAGE MAN!!

**Dungeon** The name of the Hart family basement, where Stu Hart trained his sons, Bret and Owen (as well as other wrestlers), in the craft of wrestling.

**Dwayne** This is the real first name of the most electrifying man in sports entertainment, The Rock.

**E**

**Earl Hebner** Identical twin brother of

Dave Hebner and senior official in the WWF. Similar to Dave's controversy with Hulk Hogan, it is rumored that Earl was in on the Bret Hart Screwjob at Survivor Series 1997, except this was for real.

**Elizabeth**  Truly the "First Lady" of wrestling and best known as "Macho Man" Randy Savage's savagely beautiful valet and love interest.  Remember SummerSlam 1991 "Match Made in Heaven, Match Made in Hell"? Rent it.

**Eve of Destruction**  Who needs Dick Clark and his balls? This special highlight show of 1999 aired opposite the New Year's Eve special in Times Square. At midnight Y2K Chris Jericho treated us to a cool promo.

## F

**"Fabulous Freebirds"**  Stable of the 80's whose biggest claim to fame is that one of its members is current "Jakked" commentator, Michael Hayes (aka Doc Hendricks). Hayes is also credited with helping to get the Hardy Boyz where they are today.

**Flash Funk**  This jobber of the mid-90s also went by the name 2 Cold Scorpio during his stay in WWF as well as WCW and ECW.  He was a high flyer and a pretty talented wrestler, but the Flash Funk gimmick needed A LOT of work. He would wear a silver jump suit with cowboy boots and sometimes would even have women accompany him to the ring.  Eventually the gimmick was dropped and so was Funk, despite a brief stint as part of the Job Squad with Al Snow.

**Flower Shop**  "Talk show"-like segment from wrestling past hosted by "Adorable" Adrian Adonis.  Not 100% sure why but it just didn't have the staying power of the Funeral Parlor or Pipe'rs Pit.  Perhaps it was because Adrian was a silly, out of shape, old man.

**Frankie**  Beloved pet parrot of the puffy-pantsed Koko B. Ware. Two words: High Energy.

**Frenchy Martin**  The WWF used every

French stereotype in the book to create this short-lived manager. Between his beret, long painter's smock, and mustache and goatee he was everything a person from France should be.

## G

**Gimmick Infringement** This happens when a wrestler blatantly copies the character of another. Juventud Guerrero was using the Rock's "I'm the people's champ" spiel for awhile, but no one seemed to notice. And we all remember "Bulk Bogan"....OK, we made that up.

**Greg Valentine** Nicknamed "The Hammer" this tough customer was a classic heel in the WWF from the early 80s to early 90s known for applying the figure-four leg lock on his opponents. He would also wear a shin brace, which he would move from his shin to his calf before his signature move to administer maximum pain. His best years were 1984 and 1985 in which he held the Intercontinental and Tag Team Titles (with Brutus Beefcake). Later in his career he dyed his hair jet black and joined The Honky Tonk Man in the mediocre tag team Rhythm and Blues.


**GTV** A device used to forward story lines, introduced in 1999. At the most inopportune times black and white hidden camera footage would appear on the Titantron, usually exposing some wrongdoing by someone within the federation. When it was first used it was originally titled "GDTV", and was rumored to be a new angle for the then-returning Goldust. However, Goldust was given his release from the company shortly after "GDTV" began. Since then the name was changed to "GTV" and the person(s) behind it were never revealed. We will probably never find out who the jokester is and it will go down as one of the WWF's greatest mysteries.

## H

**H-Bloxx** Band who performed a remake of Stone Cold's theme for "WWF: The Music

*"**Hurricanrana**

*Signature move of the gorgeous Lita. All the girls are doing them these days."*

Vol. 4". It was supposed to be his new theme song but didn't get much play because it was released around the time when he left to have neck surgery. When he returned he had a new song.

**Haiti Kid**  Famed midget wrestler of the late 80's, whose claim to fame was teaming with Hillbilly Jim and Little Beaver in the 6-man mixed tag match at Wrestlemania III. If the Haiti Kid can make it to Wrestlemania, there's still hope for Just Joe, right?

**Heel turn**  When a fan-favorite (face) turns to a bad guy (heel).

**Heenan Family**  This was the term used to describe all the wrestlers managed by the greatest wrestling manager of all-time, Bobby "The Brain" Heenan. Andre the Giant, Ric Flair, Rick Rude, Mr. Perfect, Haku, Lex Luger, and Arn Anderson just were some of the greats that were members of the Heenan Family, and, at the time, these were the biggest names in the business. Eventually he gave up the managerial role and moved to color commentary as part of the best broadcast team in wrestling history along side Gorilla Monsoon. Please Vince, We need the Brain back in the WWF!!!

**Hell in a Cell** This is believed to be the most dangerous match in all of wrestling. In it, a cage is placed around the outside of the ring as well as on top. Some classic Hell in a Cell matches everyone remembers are Undertaker vs. Shawn Michaels, Undertaker vs. Mankind, and Triple H vs. Cactus Jack. Some Hell in a Cell matches most people choose to forget are Undertaker vs. Big Bossman and the Kennel in a Cell match between Al Snow and the Bossman.

**"Hey, Yo"** Razor Ramons (aka Scott Hall) famous catch phrase. Always say it with a toothpick behind your ear.

**House Show** A non-televised wrestling show in which major story line advancements or title changes rarely take place. However, there are exceptions. On July 24, 1999, Edge became the new Intercontinental Champion by defeating Jeff Jarrett at a house show in Canada. Also, the Hardcore belt often changes hands at house shows due to the 24/7 rule, but it usually ends up back around the waist of the original champ.

**Hurricanrana**  Signature move of the gorgeous Lita. All the girls are doing them these days.

# I

**ICO-PRO**  Some kind of bodybuilding supplements that were heavily promoted on WWF programming in the early 90's. You remember those Bret Hart commercials for ICO-PRO dont you?

**"In Your House" PPVs**  A subtitle used for the smaller (non-big 5) pay per views introduced in the mid 90's.  This has since changed and each month now has its own permanent PPV name.  Joe attended the first "In Your House" PPV on May 15, 1995 in Syracuse, NY, where they actually gave away a house to promote the PPV. Joe didn't win.

**"Iron" Mike Sharp**  One of the WWFs most well-known jobbers. He was known for his somewhat large size, a leather forearm guard he would wear, loud yelling and grunting throughout all of his matches, and a severe lack of in-ring talent. But if you were a WWF fan in the mid to late 80's, you know "Iron" Mike.

**Irwin R. Scheister**  Aka IRS.  His real name is Mike Rotunda and went to school in our hometown of Syracuse, NY. However, he is far from a hometown hero, since probably most people that live here don't know who he is. The highlight of his career was being tag champs with Ted Dibiase as Money, Inc.

# **J**

**Jack Tunney**  The fictional WWF president occasionally appearing on WWF TV in the 80's. He would often make official announcements and make matches, much like the modern position of Commissioner. His suit and tie image was supposed to add legitimacy to the federation.

**Jameson**  Short-lived nerdy manager of the Bushwackers. We are thinking of starting a petition to get the WWF to bring back Jameson. Wanna help out? Bring a Jameson sign the next time you go to a live wrestling match. Together we can do this!

**Jean Paul**  Real first name of WWF super-star HHH. No, his first name isn't Hunter.

**Jobbers**  Oh, we do love the jobbers. Who doesnt? These are the guys who pop up on "Jakked" that youve never heard of and know are going to lose. They are usually rookies getting a shot to impress the higher-ups.

**Joey Numbers**  The all-knowing, unseen, and probably fictional pal of superstar Tazz. We don't know about you, but we hope that the WWF makes him a real character some-day.

**Jose Louis Rivera**  Another semi-famous jobber from the mid to late 80's. Nothing really special about him but he was around a lot.

**Junk Yard Dog**  Where should we start? This guy was awesome.  JYD was a staple in the 80's. Between the dog collar, chain and the word THUMP written on his ass, he was the coolest thing going at the time. If you haven't seen him, rent an old tape as soon as you can.

## K

**Kevin Kelly**  Yeah, we all know he's the chubby interview guy, but let's take a closer look.  Does he not look like a full-grown 4-year old?  Picture him in those 1930's long shorts, suspenders, a beanie cap with pro-peller, and licking a round lollipop...See what we're saying?

## L

**Lucifer**  Widely accepted as Jake's other snake, he was introduced as Damian's replacement after Jake made his triumphant return to wrestling in his morality gimmick.

**Lex Express**  In the summer of 1993 the WWF decided to make Lex Luger the next All-American hero starting with him being a surprise entrant in the Yokozuna body slam competition on the U.S.S. Intrepid. After his triumphant win, the WWF painted a tour bus and had it tour the country leading up to the SummerSlam 1993 main event of Lex vs. Yoko. Despite Lex's efforts and traveling, he never did hold WWF gold.

**Little Beaver**  This little guy is arguably the greatest midget wrestler of all time, or at least the most memorable. His shining moment was being big-splashed by the 400 lb. monster, King Kong Bundy, in a mixed six-man tag match at Wrestlemania III. I guess Bundy's partners, Little Tokyo and Lord Littlebrook, just proved too much for team.

# M

**Mae Young**  She resurfaced in 1999 to become Fabulous Moolah's partner in crime. This old chick is hardcore! At age 79 she went straight through a table and lived to tell about it.  Her best known moment was Royal Rumble 2000 where she bared her breasts on live TV. We're serious. Rent it, if you're into that sort of thing.

**Maestro/Symphony**  Well Maestro's gimmick was that of an elegant piano player, but with a fiery temper who ran Marty was a little goofy, but an amazing wrestler.

**Matilda**  The valet of one of the best tag teams in WWF history, The British Bull-dogs. No, Matilda wasn't a scantily-clad busty blond, she was a bulldog. We're not sure but we think she has died-as has the British Bulldogs career due to numerous personal problems and injuries.

*"Overselling*

*When a wrestler exaggerates the effect of his opponents' blows, such as barely getting hit with a dropkick but flying over the ropes, writhing in pain on the floor."*

**Megaphone**  This everyday object was known as the trademark of "The Mouth of the South", Jimmy Hart.  Jimmy never was at ringside without his megaphone, which he used to shout instructions to his men while they were in the ring. However, more often than not, it would end up getting thrown in the ring to help his men pull off a shady victory.

**Mid-card**  Term for wrestlers who aren't in the upper tier (like Stone Cold, the Rock, and Undertaker), but not quite bottom of the barrel either. Mid-carders generally chase the European belt and the upper mid-carders usually go for Intercontinental. Most of them hope to make the jump to Main-Eventer, however many spend their entire career chasing this goal.

**"Mine" doll**  This was the cute monster-like stuffed doll that the green-tongued, turnbuckle-eating George "The Animal" Steel carried to the ring during the last your very own "Mine" doll from the WWF catalog and at live events.

**Mr.Fuji**  We love this guy! This classic managed such greats as Demolition, Yokozuna, and The Bezerker (ok, he wasn't a great, but Fuji did manage him). Fuji was known for throwing salt in the eyes of his wrestlers' opponents, and sometimes Sesame Chicken. Did you know he's also a former tag team champion?

**Mysterious Red Liquid**  This is the term for blood, usually associated with Gangrel or the Brood.  When the Brood (Gangrel, Edge, and Christian) was still together, they would use the Red Liquid to dump on unsuspecting opponents in what was termed the "Blood Bath". Hmmm...they could call it the "Blood Bath", but couldn't call it liquid blood. What's up with that?

## N

**Nailz**  He was the antagonist in what is probably the Big Boss Man's highest pro-file feud ever. This criminal wore his prison issue orange jumpsuit to the ring, and had real bad teeth. To make him even tougher, the WWF felt the need to dub his voice with a deep robotic voice that sounded like the killer in the Scream movies. He virtually dropped out of the wrestling radar after this feud was over.

**"New" Diesel** When hugely popular Diesel (Kevin Nash) left the WWF for WCW, Vince took quite a blow. In possibly the worst decision in wrestling history, he introduced a "new" Diesel played by a never-before-seen wrestler who looked similar to Kevin. They did the same thing with Razor Ramon. Not surprisingly, poor response led to the demise of this guy. However, "New" Razor went on to become the ever-popular Kane.

**New Haircut/Old Haircut Andre** Slang term for the 2 versions of Andre the Giant figures released by LJN. They made one with short hair not long after he made his heel turn on Hulk Hogan and cut it in real life. Thus explaining the 2 toys. Duh.

# O

**Orient Express**  Kato and Tanaka formed this Mr.Fuji-led tag team. Even with Fuji at the helm, they never got the gold.

**Overselling**  When a wrestler exaggerates the effect of his opponents' blows, such as barely getting hit with a dropkick but flying over the ropes, writhing in pain on the floor.

# P

**Parts Unknown**  Used by ring announcers as the hometown of mysterious wrestlers. Most notably, the Ultimate Warrior hailed from Parts Unknown, as did pretty much every masked wrestler to ever step in the ring. Must have been a pretty happening place.

**People's Pottery**  Store found in shopping malls, that sells everything from crap made of wood, to crap made of clay, and crap made of glass.

**Pie**  Usually prefaced by "poontang". If you don't know, ask your mother.

**"Piledriver: The Album"**  One of the earlier wrestling albums of entrance themes, as well as classic performances by "Mean" Gean Okerlund, "The Doctor of Style" Slick, and Hillbilly Jim, who all sang their own songs.

**Poems on Frisbees**  Leapin Lanny Poffo used to read poems off of frisbees before his matches and then toss them out to the crowd. He later became The Genius. Lanny is the brother of Macho Man Randy Savage! Wow! He must be bitter.

**Positively Page**  We can barely look at the title and cover of this book without laughing.  An autobiography by Diamond Dallas Page, it's just one of many wrestlers' autobiographies that came out of the woodwork after the success of Mick Foley's "Have a Nice Day".

**"Preacher's Wife, The"** This was the

name of the "porn" movie Val Venis made during his feud with Goldust (then Dustin Runnels). During this time Dustin was doing a morality gimmick and was playing a preacher-type character. Thus to get under his skin, Venis had an affair with Dustin's wife Terri. Appropriately, the news was broken to Dustin through a porno movie titled "The Preacher's Wife".

**Puppies**  Simply the wrestling term for a woman's honkers or bazzongs.

**Push**  Inside lingo for when a wrestler is being promoted, or at least given a chance to succeed on a higher level. This usually comes in the form of a heel/face turn, or a feud with a high-profile star.

**Pyro**  Pyrotechnics or fireworks. You didn't actually look this one up did you?

# R

**Ric Flair Pictures**  One of the most popular abandoned story lines of all time. Ric had compromising pictures of him and the lovely Elizabeth. Macho Man refused to believe it and feuded with Flair throughout most of 1992 culminating at Wrestlemania VII. However, we never knew for sure if the pictures were real. Our theory? Of course they were real! Liz wasn't the most virtuous girl in the world. Hell, we've slept with her.

**"Rikishi Phatware"** This is the new line of clothing that Rikishi has worn since he was revealed as the driver of the car that ran down Stone Cold. So far, it seems it only consists of big-men leather suits in a variety of colors.

**Ring Rust** Term for less than stellar performances by wrestlers just returning after a long absence.

**Rockin' Wrestling** Ultra-sweet animated series starring Hulk Hogan, Roddy Piper, Junkyard Dog, and a host of other superstars. Luckily a few were released on VHS in 1999. Could a WWF animated series be successful today? Debate that with your friends.

**Russian National Anthem** Brought into American mainstream by Nikolai Volkoff as he sang it before every match. To honor this wrestling great, we will now present the lyrics in their entirety:

Note: Nikolai sang this in Russian, however, since we can't type in Russian, here it is in English. Feel free to sing along:

> *Unbreakable Union of freeborn Republics, Great Russia has welded forever to stand. Created in struggle by will of the people, United and mighty, our Soviet land!*
>
> *Sing to the Motherland, home of the free, Bulwark of peoples in*

*brotherhood strong. O
Party of Lenin, the
strength of the people,
To Communism's
triumph lead us on!*

*Through tempests the
sunrays of freedom
have cheered us, Along
the new path where
great Lenin did lead.
To a righteous cause he
raised up the peoples,
Inspired them to labor
and valorous deed.*

*Sing to the Motherland,
home of the free,
Bulwark of peoples in
brotherhood strong. O
Party of Lenin, the
strength of the people,
To Communism's
triumph lead us on!*

*In the vict'ry of*

*Communism's death-*
*less ideal,*
*We see the future of our*
*dear land.*
*And to her fluttering*
*scarlet banner, Self-*
*lessly true we always*
*shall stand!*

## <u>S</u>

**"Saving Ryan's Privates"** Another porn movie made by Val Venis during his feud with Ken Shamrock. In this movie, Val appeared with Ken's on-screen sister, Ryan, in the shower. Shammy was not too happy with Val or his sister and thus furthered their feud.

**Sell** Acting in pain to make an opponent's attack believable. See "overselling".

**"Sensational" Sherri** Sherri was the original heel valet of the late 80's and early 90's. She began as a wrestler, but due to lack of competition and the fact that no one cared about women's wrestling at the time, she turned to managing. Most notably, she was Macho Man's woman for a while during his time as a heel, however he eventually turned face and returned to Elizabeth. After that she managed a newly-turned heel, Shawn Michaels, and led him to Intercontinental gold.

**Shoot**  As you know, wrestling is scripted, thus a shoot is any move, action, or dialogue done by wrestlers that's NOT in the script.  They can get into serious trouble for on-air unscripted comments. Watch Kevin Nash in almost every promo he cuts in WCW, pretty much every word he says is a shoot (usually degrading the company).

**Shotgun Saturday Night**  Former name of what is now "Jakked".  With Michael Hayes and Jonathan Coachman on commentary, this show basically recaps "Raw" and "Smackdown".  It also has low profile matches with up-and-coming athletes.

**Skinner** Wild tobacco-spewing rogue from

the Australian Outback. At the time, Crocodile Dundee was tearing up the box office, so the WWF decided to play off of that. Many believe Paul Hogan himself would have been more skilled in the ring. He cut a mean promo though.

**Smash figure**  In the huge line of Hasbro WWF toys in the 90's, Ax and Smash of Demolition were available separately. Later on when Crush was introduced to eventually replace Ax, the only way to get his figure was in a 2 pack with Smash! Of course, any real fan already had Smash. Thus having 2 Smashs in your collection is a good gauge of how die-hard you were.

**Spanish Announce Table**  This thing used to get broken every week!  It's been on hiatus from the weekly TV shows lately, but you can count on it being at every Pay-Per-View.  I bet those Spanish announcers make some killer calls.

**Stinkface**  This move will go down as one of the most disgusting moves in all of

*"Three I's*

*Popular creed of WWF superstar Kurt Angle. Intensity, Integrity, and Intelligence."*

wrestling history, next to the Pit Stop and the Bronco Buster. Made famous by Rikishi, this 400-lb man in a thong would rub his ass into his opponent's face. Makes a chokeslam from the Big Show sound pretty appealing, huh?

**Stu and Helen** - Bret and Owen Hart's mom and pop. Many of the greats trained with Stu including Chris Jericho and Chris Benoit. Practically the whole Hart family tree is involved in the business.

# T

**Tag Ropes** These things are from waaaaaaaaay back! In tag matches, the wrestler on the apron had to be holding a white rope tied to the turnbuckle in order to receive a valid tag.

**Tammy Lynn Sytch** Real name of famed WWF Diva Sunny. This girl can't hold a job to save her life! She's worked on and off for every major promotion. Notorious for auctioning her breast implants on the Internet. You'd think after all these years in wrestling, she'd be financially secure enough so that wouldn't be necessary. She is also the wife of Chris Candito (aka Skip) who had a brief stint in the WWF as well.

**Ted Arcidi**  Nothing much to say here, just a real tough guy from the mid-80's. Joe has his LJN action figure. Also he is rumored to be the man who got Triple H into the business.

**Team Extreme**  Unofficial group name of the Hardy Boyz and Lita.

**Texas Tornado**  (Real name Kerry Von Erich) Kerry stormed into the WWF in the early 90's in hopes of making it big, which he may have if not for his untimely death. Kerry and his four brothers were trained to wrestle by their father Fritz Von Erich. After three of his brothers died (two of them committing suicide), Kerry also ended his life by shooting himself in the chest in 1993. On a lighter note, he held the Intercontinental Title in the WWF and has a cameo role in the 1990 hit movie "Problem Child".

**Three I's**  Popular creed of WWF superstar Kurt Angle. Intensity, Integrity, and Intelligence.

**Three Ninjas: High Noon At Mega Mountain**  OK, first off this is the 4th 3 Ninjas film! WHO in Hollywood greenlighted a FOURTH 3 Ninjas film?  Everyone knows the franchise lost all credibility after the forgettable" 3Ninjas: Kick Back". As if starring Hulk Hogan as Dave Dragon wasn't painful enough, NOT ONE of the 3 Ninjas from the original movie reprised their roles as Rocky, Colt, and the lovable Tum Tum! Can you blame them?

**Tito Santana**  The quintessential Intercontinental Champion during the 80's. He got SO much airtime, we can't remember watching Saturday mornings and NOT seeing him! As his popularity dwindled he re-invented himself by playing off his Mexican origin as El Matador, the wrestler slash bullfighter.

**Tony Chimel**  Long-time ring announcer of the WWF, usually working the Smackdown broadcasts. Fun Fact: Famed Ring Announcer Howard "The Fink" Finkel was the first employee the company ever hired, and he's still with them today.

## U

**"Under Creative Development"** Term used when the team of writers are trying to come up with a new story line or persona for a wrestler. Many times when a crappy wrestler is off TV, this is the excuse they use.

**Urn** Hello! When Undertaker first arrived, his manager Paul Bearer carried a large urn to ringside. It somehow empowered the Taker and led him to many victories. Maybe Essa Rios should get an urn.

## V

**Vader** Big, bulky guy who wrestled for a million different promotions. He had moderate success in the WWF but his true claim to fame was being the man Mick Foley was facing when he lost his right ear.

**Vignettes** Promotional video clips shown before the debut of a new wrestler. Can also be used to describe any scene with out of ring interaction between wrestlers. We think that everyone should agree that "Mr. Perfect", Curt Hennig, did the best examples of these in the early 90's. Who could top Curt passing a football to himself across an entire football field or making a full-court basket. Simply Perfect!

**Virgil** The tough bodyguard of "Million Dollar Man", Ted Dibiase. During his tenure as bodyguard, fans noticed his huge arms and figured he'd be amazing in the ring if given the chance. Well his day came, and well...he probably should have kept the bodyguard gig. He then left the WWF to become "Vincent" in WCW.

## W

**Warlord**  Mid-carder from the late 80's who was originally part of the Powers of Pain with The Barbarian. They enjoyed great success in the few months before the Legion of Doom entered the federation and basically took their spot. The Powers were then split up and Warlord got a new gimmick. He dressed in all black, had a mask covering half his face, a staff with a huge "W", and was managed by Slick. We firmly believe all wrestlers should carry their own monogramed staff today.

**WBF**  (World Bodybuilding Federation) This was an extremely lame venture by Vince McMahon that basically showcased muscle-bound men flexing the entire show. He was young then, we all make mistakes. They even had a Pay-Per-View for the championship. If you ordered that, you are truly a hardcore Vince fan.

**Where to \_\_\_\_\_-anie???**  Our favorite WWF quote in recent memory!  After luring a sweet young Stephanie into his limo, the Undertaker turned around from the driver's seat...in his most menacing voice he screamed "WHERE TO STEPHANIE!??! It was HILARIOUS!!! Not long after he put her on a cross, tried to sacrifice her, and make her his wife.  Pretty standard stuff.

**Wonders of the World**  In reality there are seven of these that include the Taj Mahal and the Pyramids of Egypt.  Beyond those wrestling fans know that there are actually an 8th and 9th.  Andre the Giant was billed as the eight wonder of the world due to his extremely large size. More recently, Chyna has added herself to this list by being named the 9th wonder of the world for her strength and size.  We think it's really because she looks a hell of a lot like a man but really is a woman. You be the judge.

**Wrestle Vessle**  This is so funny to us, although if given the opportunity we'd be on it in a second!  Just picture a regular cruise, except with Test signing pictures at a long table. That's pretty much how we think it is.  Makes a great honeymoon trip. "Honey, I know your heart was set on Hawaii, but I think I've planned something you'll like EVEN more..."

# The Authors

Matt Hiller was born September 28, 1977 in Syracuse, New York, to rave reviews. He leaves home rarely, except to attend a WWF show.

Being a professional comedy writer, however, Matt finds it necessary to work at a popular clothing store in order to keep himself in luxury items - like food. Though battling a crush on Stephanie McMahon, Matt is still single.

A few years ago Matt teamed up with his lifelong friend, Joe Lisi, to create a sketch-comedy cable access show called "Frobbin Around," filled with outlandish skits and crazy stunts including 2 minutes of rapidly blinking light patterns set to the "Barney" theme song. They were embraced as sort of local icons for these types of antics. Really.

Matt started watching wrestling when he was about 5, eventually becoming obsessed with it as he progressed through his teen years, to what is probably a full-blown behavioral disorder at present. This book came about quite unintentionally when Matt and Joe began e-mailing one-liners to each other for their own amusement. After Matt realized they had written about three hundred of these gems he stood up from his chair and screamed, "WE MUST BRING THIS TO THE MASSES!" And so he did.

Matt hopes you "bust your leg laughing". If you'd like to contact Matt for any reason, or if you are Stephanie McMahon, please send an e-mail to dillpup@yahoo.com.

Now go read the book!

**Matt Hiller**

Joe Lisi is 23 years old and has lived in Syracuse, New York his entire life. After meeting Matt on the bus in eighth grade he quickly discovered that not only did they both have cool Bart Simpson hats with buttons on them (it WAS 1990, guys) but they were both funny. Through the rest of high school Joe and Matt honed their skills writing off-beat, quirky comedy material.

Despite the experience of having his high school burned down by a fellow student (every kid's dream became reality!), Joe thrived and graduated. Between his job and college work he collaborated with Matt to co-write and co-star in the hit cable access comedy show, "Frobbin' Around."

Needless to say, wrestling has been a huge part of Joe's life. Frankly, he's a way bigger and more knowledgeable wrestling fan than you could ever aspire to be. To give you an idea of how die-hard Joe is he still owns and uses a WWF pillowcase.

Joe took a break from watching wrestling regularly from 1995-1998, but couldn't stay away for long. Since having weekly parties to watch wrestling, eat pizza and go mad with Matt and their friend, Brian, he's gotten back into the game and is once again completely addicted, never missing a show.

Oh, and Joe loves his his action figures! Don't touch his Triple H or he'll ruin your life!

**Joe Lisi**

Printed in the United States
4764